I Wonder
Which Snake Is The Longest

• • • • • • • • • • • • • • • • •

and other neat facts about animal records

By Annabelle Donati
Illustrated by Pamela G. Johnson

A GOLDEN BOOK • NEW YORK
Western Publishing Company, Inc.
Racine, Wisconsin 53404

Produced by Graymont Enterprises, Inc., Norfolk, Connecticut
Producer: *Ruth Lerner Perle*
Design: *Michele Italiano-Perla*
Editorial consultant: *Penny Kalk*, New York Zoological Society,
Bronx, N.Y.

Contents

Which animal is the largest of all?

The blue whale is the largest living animal. In fact, it is probably the largest animal that has ever lived on this planet, including the largest dinosaurs! The blue whale can grow to be more than one hundred feet long—the length of six automobiles lined up in a row. It can weigh an amazing two hundred tons. That's almost as much as fifty elephants!

Tell Me More

Whales are mammals, not fish. Although they live in the water, they must come up to the surface to breathe air. And like all mammals, the females produce milk for their babies. Blue whales feed in the cold oceans near the North and South poles and travel to the warm, tropical seas to mate.

Weight watcher

A blue whale's heart weighs one thousand pounds. Its tongue weighs more than six thousand pounds. And its bones weigh fifteen thousand pounds.

Big blue beauty

Even though the blue whale is huge, it can swim fast—more than thirty miles per hour. It can leap out of the water and swim on its back. It can dive fifteen hundred feet and stay underwater for as long as an hour and a half before coming up for air.

How does this giant eat?

The blue whale has no teeth. It feeds only on *plankton*, which are very small plants, and tiny shrimplike creatures called *krill*. Each day, this huge animal eats more than ten thousand pounds of plankton. It filters the plankton through a strainer system of thin, bony "plates" in its mouth. These plates are called *baleen*.

Largest eye

Despite the blue whale's size, its eyes are only four inches across. The giant squid holds the record for the largest eye—fifteen inches across. This is larger than a dinner plate!

Bouncing baby whales

Blue whales are not only the largest but also among the fastest-growing animals on earth. When born, the blue whale is twenty-three feet long and weighs about two thousand pounds. The mother whale feeds her baby thick, nutritious milk forty times a day, and the baby gains almost nine pounds every hour! By the time the young whale is a year old, it weighs fifty thousand pounds—more than ten times its birth weight.

Which land animal is the biggest?

Elephants are the largest animals to walk the earth. African elephants can be up to thirteen feet tall at the shoulder and weigh as much as twenty-two thousand pounds. These lumbering giants have always been a source of wonder, thanks partly to their amazing trunks and tusks and their great strength and intelligence. But it is probably their enormous size that makes them so fascinating to us.

How big is the baby?

The newborn baby elephant is about three feet tall and weighs about two hundred forty pounds. The calf grows quickly. By the time it is three years old, the young elephant tips the scales at more than two thousand pounds.

Amazing *but* TRUE

An elephant never stops growing. The older it gets, the bigger it gets. So the largest elephant in a herd is also usually the oldest.

Vegetarian

An elephant does not eat meat. It feeds mostly on plants. Each day, this huge animal eats more than five hundred pounds of plants. It also drinks about forty gallons of water. That's more than six hundred cupfuls!

Measuring up

An elephant's trunk, which is both its nose and its mouth, weighs about three hundred pounds. The trunk is strong enough to pull branches from trees, yet delicate enough to pick up a peanut with its sensitive tip. The animal's large, thin ears can measure five feet long and four feet wide.

An elephant's tusks, which are ivory, never stop growing. The tusk of an older male elephant can weigh more than two hundred pounds. This is why hunters who illegally kill elephants for their valuable ivory prefer to go after older males.

Tell Me More

An elephant can walk, swim, and run, but it cannot jump. Its thick, straight legs act as pillars to support its heavy body. Its large padded feet help it move quietly through the underbrush, leaving hardly any track marks.

Which mammal is the smallest?

Kitti's hog-nosed bat, also known as the bumblebee bat, is the tiniest mammal in the animal kingdom. It is only one inch long and weighs just one-twentieth of an ounce—less than a dime. Like all mammals, the female gives birth to a live baby and produces milk. And like other bats, this tiny creature can flap its wings and fly like a bird. A thin but tough layer of skin is connected to the bat's long, bony fingers, arms, legs, and toes. This skin forms the wings.

Tell Me More

The bumblebee bat's wingspan is about six inches. That's a lot of wing for a tiny animal!

What does the bumblebee bat eat?

Like most bats, bumblebee bats, which live in Asia, rest during the day. They hang upside down in caves. But at night, when it is safer for them to hunt, they spread their wings and search for insects such as beetles.

How do bats see at night?

Although some bats can see quite well, most bats, like the bumblebee bat, have poor eyesight. However, all bats have a keen sense of hearing. Bats also have a special system of finding their way in the dark. They produce high-pitched clicks and listen for the echoes. This helps them locate prey and keeps them from bumping into objects in their path.

Smallest bird

The Cuban bee hummingbird is the smallest bird. It weighs even less than the bumblebee bat. It is about the size of a bumblebee and, like a bee, drinks nectar from flowers.

Which animal is the strongest?

It's not an elephant. It's not a bear. It's a beetle! The rhinoceros beetle, which lives in South America, is the strongest of all animals. This amazing insect can lift eight hundred fifty times its own weight. If you were as strong as this beetle, you would be able to lift three elephants—a combined weight of about twenty-seven thousand pounds!

How is this beetle like a rhinoceros?

The rhinoceros beetle is a longhorn beetle. It has feelers on its head that look like rhinoceros horns. The male uses his "horns" for fighting with other beetles or for showing off.

Tell Me More

The rhinoceros beetle, like all adult beetles, has two sets of wings. Tough outer wings fold neatly over delicate flying wings. These outer wings serve as armor to protect the beetle's softer underparts.

Which animal is the tallest?

When it comes to height, the giraffe is the earth's undisputed champion. This gentle and graceful animal measures more than nineteen feet tall from the tips of its toes to the tops of its skin-covered horns. A giraffe is already well over six feet tall when it is born—about as tall as the average professional basketball player. By the time the giraffe is four years old, it has reached its full adult height.

Odd companions

Tiny oxpeckers, or tickbirds, often ride on the giraffe's neck and back. These birds eat ticks and remove dirt and bits of dry skin from the giraffe's neck and body.

Chomping champ

When the giraffe stretches its long neck, it can reach to the top of a twenty-foot-high acacia tree. With the help of its long tongue, which can grasp leaves and branches, the giraffe eats one hundred twenty-five pounds of food a day.

High kicker

The giraffe's legs are long and strong. One kick from a giraffe's hind leg can kill an adult lion.

Traveling tower

Giraffes often travel across the plains of Africa with zebras and antelope. Giraffes can see over the heads of these smaller animals and so spot danger first. When the other animals see the giraffes start to run, they know that they, too, had better take off.

Pretty patterns

Giraffes from different regions of Africa have different markings and colors. As with human fingerprints, no two giraffes have exactly the same markings.

Nifty nostrils

Unlike most other animals, the giraffe can open and close its nostrils.

Light sleeper

When a giraffe sleeps, it twists its neck around and rests its head on its hindquarters. It sleeps for about five minutes at a time.

Although the giraffe's neck is almost seven feet long, it has the same number of bones as a human being's—seven. Of course, each bone is much larger than the equivalent human bone.

Which snake is the longest?

The longest of all snakes is probably the reticulated python, which lives in the jungles of southeastern Asia. It can grow up to thirty-three feet long—about the length of six adult humans laid end to end. This powerful giant is also known for the beautiful pattern on its skin.

Is the python poisonous?

No. The python is a *constrictor*. This means that it wraps its body around its victim and squeezes until the prey is crushed or suffocated. The snake then lets go of its victim and devours it.

The python can unhinge its jaws and open its mouth wide enough to swallow its prey whole. After a big meal, it can go for many weeks without eating.

What do pythons eat?

Pythons love to eat jungle cats, but they will also feed on smaller animals, such as monkeys or pigs. They rarely attack people. But people often kill pythons for their tasty meat and beautiful skin.

Tell Me More

Scientists believe that snakes of long ago could walk. Pythons have tiny stubs on their underparts, called *vestigial legs*. These may be all that is left of what were once true legs.

Mother care

Unlike most snakes, the reticulated python mother guards her eggs. She coils her body around them and rests her head on top until the babies are ready to hatch.

One reticulated python that lived in a zoo didn't eat for nineteen months. Then it ate and fasted again—this time for seventeen months.

Heavyweight champion

The heaviest of all snakes—some scientists say it is also the longest—is the anaconda, which lives in South America. Most anacondas grow to be about twenty-five feet long. But the largest one on record was thirty-seven feet long and weighed more than a thousand pounds. Because it is so heavy, the anaconda spends much of its time in water, which supports its great weight.

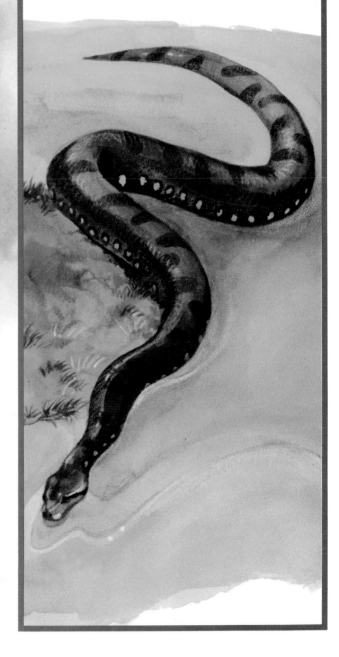

Which animal is the noisiest?

The howler monkey is the loudest animal living on land. Its eerie bark can be heard for more than ten miles in the forests of Central and South America.

Louder than a dog's bark, a donkey's bray, or a wolf's howl, this monkey's cry echoes throughout the forest, calling its group, or *troop*, together and warning other monkeys to stay away. The howling usually begins at daybreak, when other forest creatures start wandering into the howler's neighborhood.

How does the howler make such a loud sound?

The howler monkey has an extra-large bone in its throat. Pushing air through a hollow space in this bone can produce an earsplitting noise. Males are much noisier than females.

Do howler monkey troops fight?

Not really. When two troops meet, they howl and make faces at each other. But eventually they go their own ways without fighting.

Tell Me More

Howler monkeys climb trees and walk on land. But they don't swim across rivers. As a result, howler troops on opposite banks of the same river don't usually mix and may look very different from each other. There are six different kinds of howler monkey.

The blue whale's "song" travels even farther than the howler monkey's call. It can be heard through the water over a distance of more than five hundred miles.

Which animal has the longest lifespan?

The giant tortoise of the Galápagos Islands in the Pacific Ocean and the Aldabra tortoise of the Seychelles island group in the Indian Ocean are believed to live more than one hundred fifty years. This is longer than any other animal with a backbone.

Galápagos tortoises are among the largest tortoises. They weigh up to five hundred pounds and have a shell that is about four feet long.

Are Galápagos tortoises dangerous?

No. Galápagos tortoises are so gentle that children ride them in zoos.

Water routes

Galápagos tortoises live near the sea but make regular trips to the hills for drinking water. These tortoises have taken the same routes for hundreds of years. As a result, the stones on the paths they use are worn and polished. When people on the islands need fresh water, they often follow these shiny stones.

Amazing but TRUE

Every evening, Galápagos tortoises travel to their sleeping grounds in a definite order. Each goes to the same resting place it used the night before. In the morning, too, the tortoises leave in order—but not in the same order in which they came!

Which bird is the fastest flyer?

The spine-tailed swift of eastern Asia can travel faster than any other living thing on earth. This small bird can fly along a straight path at more than one hundred miles per hour. Some scientists believe that when the swift travels with the wind, it can fly much faster than that.

Steep steppers

Since the swift's feet are too small to hold on to branches, the bird builds its nest in hollow trees and along the sides of rocks and tree trunks. Its wing feathers have tiny hooks that help it cling to these surfaces. Spines at the end of its tail feathers help the bird brace itself.

Tell Me More

Combining wingbeats and short glides, swifts can stay in the air for very long periods of time. These amazing birds can do almost everything while flying: catch and eat insects, mate, and collect materials for their nests.

Fastest diver

The peregrine falcon, found in North and South America, Australia, and Africa, can dive through the air at one hundred seventy-five miles per hour. That's faster than any other bird can dive.

17

Which animal is the fastest runner?

The cheetah, that graceful, spotted African cat, can run at a rate of sixty-five miles per hour. That's faster than the speed limit on most American highways. But the cheetah can maintain its record-breaking speed for only a short distance—about the length of four city blocks. Therefore, when it spots its prey, such as an impala or a gazelle, the cheetah creeps up as close as it can before it takes off after the other animal.

How can the cheetah run so fast?

Every part of this cat's body is built for speed. The cheetah has a small skull and a sleek frame with hardly any fat on it. Its long, muscular hind legs and flexible spine allow it to take long strides. The cheetah uses its tail to steer and balance itself, and its exposed claws give the animal a good grip on the ground as it runs.

Va-room!

The cheetah accelerates like a sports car. From a full-stop position, it usually takes a cheetah less than a minute to catch its prey.

When does the cheetah hunt?

The cheetah usually hunts during the day, when other wild cats are asleep. But it doesn't always start eating right away. Instead, it carries its kill to a hiding place, where it won't have to share with other animals.

Royal cats

Cheetahs have been a symbol of grace and power for thousands of years. Egyptian pharaohs, Russian princes, and Mongolian emperors kept cheetahs as pets and took them along when they went hunting.

Marked

The cheetah's coat has a pattern of small black spots on a tawny yellow background. Its face has a pair of dark stripes that run from the eyes down the sides of its nose.

Tell Me More

Cheetahs are not long-distance runners. The North American pronghorn antelope is the fastest runner for the longest period of time. This antelope can sustain a speed of forty-five miles per hour for a distance of more than four miles.

Which fish is the fastest swimmer?

The magnificent sailfish holds the world record for speed swimming. At almost seventy miles per hour, this fish swims even faster than the fastest land animal—the cheetah—can run.

The sailfish is found in the warmer waters of both the Pacific and Atlantic oceans. Small scales give its streamlined body—shaped like a torpedo—a smooth, shiny surface for easy gliding through the water.

Does the sailfish really have a sail?

The huge "sail" is really a large fin on the fish's back. It helps the fish steer and cut through the water. To swim fast, the sailfish neatly folds this fin into a groove on its back.

Tell Me More

The female sailfish lays as many as five million eggs at a time. The eggs float on the water. Not many hatch, however, because birds and other fish like to eat them.

The sailfish's long, narrow beak is very sharp and strong. In fact, it can pierce right through the sides of some boats.

Which mammal is the slowest creeper?

The three-toed sloth, or ai, which lives in the rainforests of South America, is the slowest mammal on earth. It hardly ever moves, and when it does, it rarely creeps faster than ten feet per hour. Although it is as large as a house cat, this animal doesn't travel much faster than a snail, which is a mollusk and the slowest animal on earth.

Why doesn't the sloth fall off the tree?

The three-toed sloth eats, sleeps, and even gives birth while hanging upside down from a tree. Its long, curved claws hook on to a branch and don't let go. Its grip is so strong that the sloth sometimes continues to hold on to the branch even after it has died.

Mossy

Although the ai's natural coloring is gray and brown, green plants called *algae* grow on the sloth's fur. This makes the animal look like a clump of moss hanging from a tree branch. The unmoving sloth can hardly be seen among the leaves. Predators often pass right by and do not even know it is there.

Amazing but TRUE

The hair on the three-toed sloth grows away from the body in many directions. Although this may make the animal look untidy, it has an important use: to allow rainwater to easily run off the sloth's body while hanging upside down.

Tell Me More

The sloth's legs are not designed for standing or walking. Its long, curved claws get in the way. On the rare occasions when this animal is on the forest floor, it drags its body along the ground.

Which animal is the highest jumper?

The tiny flea is one of nature's greatest athletes. This insect can leap more than three hundred times the length of its body. If you could do that, you would be able to get from one end of a football field to the other in a single hop.

Wingless wonder

A flea has no wings. But it has extremely powerful muscles in its hind legs that can propel it into the air. In addition, near its legs the flea produces an elastic substance that makes the legs work like a snapping rubber band. This gives the tiny insect an extra push. A flea often turns a somersault in the course of a jump.

What is a flea circus?

Years ago, some people used thin gold wires to attach fleas to miniature wagons and trains. Because their legs were so powerful, the fleas were able to move these objects and perform other tricks. Their owners claimed that the fleas were trained acrobats, but the tiny insects were merely trying to jump away.

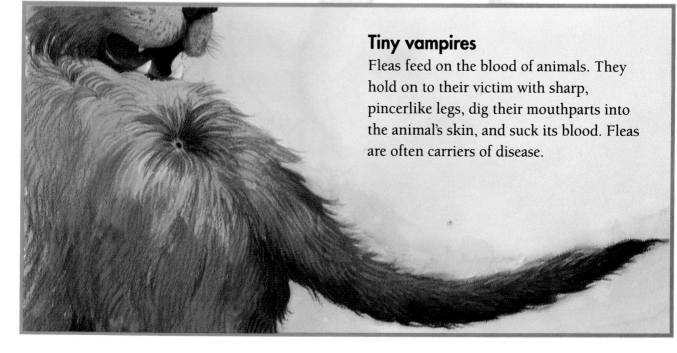

Tiny vampires

Fleas feed on the blood of animals. They hold on to their victim with sharp, pincerlike legs, dig their mouthparts into the animal's skin, and suck its blood. Fleas are often carriers of disease.

Which mammal is the deepest diver?

Some years ago a sperm whale was caught that had a shark in its stomach. This type of shark lives at the bottom of the ocean—more than ten thousand feet down. This is why some scientists believe that the sperm whale holds the record for deep diving.

However, many other scientists think that the giant elephant seal is the world's diving champion. This largest of all seals is found off the coasts of California, Mexico, and South America. It can dive three to four thousand feet in its search for squid, fish, and crabs near the bottom of the ocean. It takes only seventeen minutes for this remarkable animal to reach that depth.

Fast food

Elephant seals spend months at sea feeding and building up a layer of fat called *blubber*. When the seals finally come on land to breed, they don't eat or drink for three months. Instead, they live on their storehouse of blubber.

Amazing *but* TRUE

Unlike most other mammals, the female elephant seal sheds her old coat of fur and the top layer of her skin when breeding season is over. A new coat soon grows in.

Does the elephant seal have a trunk?

It doesn't have a real trunk. But the male, or bull, does have a large nose, which hangs over his mouth. Sometimes he blows up this nose like a balloon and makes a loud sound with it to show his mate how powerful he is. He also blows up his snout to frighten others away. The roar of a big bull may carry for miles.

Which bird has the widest wingspan?

When the wandering albatross's wings are spread out, they measure almost twelve feet from tip to tip. This wingspan is wider than that of any other bird. Surprisingly, these wings are quite narrow—only ten inches across. This magnificent bird can be seen soaring and gliding gracefully on the air currents of the South Pacific Ocean.

Old salt

The wandering albatross loves to fly over the ocean. It often stays at sea for months at a time, catching fish in its strong, hooked beak and drinking seawater. It can travel for miles without flapping its wings.

Where does the albatross sleep?

The albatross is quite comfortable sleeping on the surface of the water.

Precious baby

The mother albatross lays only one egg every two years. For two months the mother and father take turns sitting on the egg. Because they have so few babies, protecting the chick is especially important to the parents.

The stomach of the adult albatross produces a foul-smelling liquid that the bird feeds to its baby. When a young albatross feels threatened, it spits this liquid at its enemy, causing the intruder to flee.

Amazing but TRUE

In the insect kingdom, the Queen Alexandra bird-wing, a butterfly, has the largest wingspan. Its wings, tip to tip, measure more than eleven inches.

Champion long-distance flyer

Although the albatross has the longest wings, the much smaller arctic tern is the champion long-distance flyer. Each year, it flies all the way from the North Pole (the Arctic) to the South Pole (the Antarctic) and back again. It takes the tern only two months to fly almost twenty-five thousand miles. This is the distance each way. And it can fly more than fourteen thousand miles nonstop.

Sound off!

The albatross has an unusual call that sounds very much like a donkey's bray.

Tell Me More

Before mating, albatross couples throw back their heads and circle around each other. They point their bills and huge wings toward the sky and sing "love songs" to each other. Finally, they give each other gifts of sticks. Albatross pairs stay together for life.

Which mammal has the most babies?

Monkeys, elephants, cows, and horses each have one baby at a time or, at most, two babies. Dogs and cats usually have litters of six, seven, or sometimes eight. But the tailless tenrec usually has at least fifteen babies and sometimes more than thirty! No other mammal has so many babies at one time.

What is a tailless tenrec?

The shrewlike tenrec, from the island of Madagascar, looks a little like a hedgehog. As its name suggests, it has no tail. It is about the size of a mouse and has a long, pointed snout and sharp teeth. Its coat of hair is short and bristly, with long, thin spines that run along the animal's back. These spines stand up when the tenrec feels threatened. The tenrec also snorts, grunts, spits, and hisses to scare enemies away.

Tell Me More

During the day, the tenrec rests in rocky crags, ground holes, or dug-out burrows. It comes out at dusk to search for food. Using its claws and long, pointy snout, it digs for insects, worms, and sometimes snails. The tenrec also eats lizard eggs, fruits, and berries.

Tenrec babies need a lot of nourishment. So the mother sometimes takes her young out during the daytime to look for food. The striped coat and dull colors of the babies help them blend in with their surroundings. As the young tenrecs grow, their coat changes, and they lose their protective coloring.

Amazing but TRUE

In the winter, when there are few insects to be found, the tenrec digs into its underground burrow. It rolls up into a ball, with its nose between its paws. Then it closes its eyes, slows its breathing, and stops moving. In this state of rest, called *hibernation*, the tenrec can go without food for more than five months.

Which animal is the most intelligent?

Most creatures in the animal kingdom have at least some inborn knowledge, called *instinct*. But instinct is different from intelligence. Intelligence is the ability to reason and solve problems. Elephants, dolphins, whales, and pigs can all reason and solve problems, but the chimpanzee, which lives in Africa, is more intelligent than any of them. With the exception of human beings, the chimpanzee—especially the pygmy chimp, or bonobo—is the most intelligent animal.

Canny communicators

Scientists who study animal behavior have taught chimpanzees to communicate by using sign language. In addition to being able to create words and sentences, some of these chimps have learned to count, identify shapes, and solve simple puzzles.

Tool toters

The clever chimpanzee makes and uses a variety of tools, such as the ones below, in its search for food.

Ant catcher: This is a simple but effective tool for getting ants out of the ground. The chimp strips leaves off a stick or stem to make it smooth. Then it lowers the stick into an ant nest and waits. When the ants crawl up the stick, the chimp quickly licks them up.

Leaf sponge: To get drinking water out of a rain-soaked rock, the chimpanzee sticks a special kind of leaf inside cracks in the rock. The leaf soaks up the water. Then the chimp sucks the water out of the leaf.

Bed makers

Every night, the chimpanzee weaves fresh branches and leaves together to make a cozy bed up in the trees. It takes a chimp less than ten minutes to make its bed.

Smart soldiers

Chimpanzees guard the borders of their territory by wielding sticks and throwing stones. A rock-throwing chimp can hit an animal such as a pig, an antelope, or a monkey from up to fifteen feet away. If intruders attack, the "border patrol" acts as a team. Some of the chimps hold the intruders while others bite and hit them. Chimpanzees also throw rocks and stones to show off.

Fruit and nut crackers: **The chimp uses heavy sticks and stones to smash food items that have a hard shell or skin.**

Honey holers: **Sticks are used by the chimp to enlarge the holes in beehives. This makes gathering honey simpler.**

Tell Me More

Although you have come to the last page of this book, you are only beginning to learn about the champions of the animal kingdom. Even if it is not a record holder, each animal—be it large or small, fast or slow—has some special advantage that helps it survive in the wild.

There seems to be a plan for everything in nature. Each plant and animal has a role to fulfill. Each has an effect on something else that sooner or later has an effect on us.

Here are some more amazing-but-true facts about animal record holders to start you on your way to new discoveries:

- The slowest-growing animal is the deep-sea clam. It takes one hundred years for it to grow to its full size—less than half an inch.

- The millipede has several hundred legs—more than any other animal.

- The shortest-lived animal is the mayfly, which lives just one day as an adult.

- The bird-eating spider is the largest of all spiders. Its web is strong enough to trap birds, mice, and other small animals.

- The smallest of all creatures are the protozoa. These are so tiny, in fact, that they can be seen only through a microscope.

- The whale shark is the largest fish. It lays the biggest eggs, too—twelve inches long and five inches at their widest point.

- When it is born, the ocean sunfish is one tenth of an inch long and weighs just a fraction of an ounce. When fully grown, some of these fish are ten feet long and weigh over five thousand pounds. No other fish that small at birth grows to be so big.